O9-AHW-831

A WICKED HISTORY™

# Alexander the Great

## Master of the Ancient World

DOUG WILHELM

Franklin Watts®
An Imprint of Scholastic Inc.
New York   Toronto   London   Auckland   Sydney
Mexico City   New Delhi   Hong Kong
Danbury, Connecticut

# The World of Alexander the Great

In 11 years of brilliant and brutal conquest, Alexander built one of the largest empires the world had ever seen.

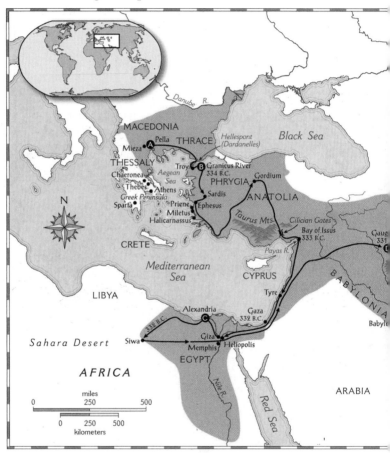

*Stillness and silence born of fear
held fast all who were in his presence. For he was
intolerable, and murderous, reputed in fact
to be melancholy mad.*

Ancient Greek historian Ephippus
of Olynthus, about Alexander the Great

## To Nate (the Great)

Photographs © 2010: akg-Images, London: 51 (Peter Connolly), 19, 78 top, 116; Art Resource, NY: 83 bottom (Alinari/Museo Archeologico Nazionale, Naples), 10 (Alinari/Museo Barracco, Rome), 26 (HIP/Ann Ronan Picture Library, London), 82 bottom, 95 (HIP/British Library, London), 63 (Kavaler/Louvre, Paris), 87 (Erich Lessing/Louvre, Paris), 60, 61 (Erich Lessing/Pinacoteca Capitolina, Musei Capitolini, Rome); Bridgeman Art Library International Ltd., London/New York: 78 right (Giraudon/Louvre, Paris), 65 (Giraudon/Musee de la Ville de Paris/Musee du Petit-Palais), 48 (Giraudon/Musee Lambinet, Versailles/Lauros), 119 (Giraudon/Museo Archeologico Nazionale, Naples); Corbis Images: 28, 33, 78 bottom left, 79 top right, 81 bottom, 114 (Bettmann), 82 top (Diego Lezama Orezzoli); Getty Images: 47, 79 bottom, 80 center (Hulton Archive), 106 (Tom Lovell/National Geographic), 40 (Picture Post), 82 center (Stock Montage); Mary Evans Picture Library: 81 top (Douglas McCarthy), 54, 76, 77, 83 center; North Wind Picture Archives: 14, 29, 38, 68, 72, 80 top, 80 bottom, 81 center, 83 top, 90, 98, 100, 117; Stock Montage, Inc.: 70; The Granger Collection, New York: 23, 79 center, 93.

**Illustrations by XNR Productions, Inc.: 4, 5, 8, 9**
**Cover art, page 8 inset by Mark Summers**
**Chapter art by Raphael Montoliu**

Library of Congress Cataloging-in-Publication Data
Wilhelm, Doug.
Alexander the Great : master of the ancient world / Doug Wilhelm.
p. cm. — (A wicked history)
Includes bibliographical references and index.
ISBN-13: 978-0-531-21275-2 (lib. bdg.) 978-0-531-22821-0 (pbk.)
ISBN-10: 0-531-21275-0 (lib. bdg.) 0-531-22821-5 (pbk.)
1. Alexander, the Great, 356–323 B.C.—Juvenile literature. 2. Greece—History—Macedonian Expansion, 359–323 B.C.—Juvenile literature. 3. Generals—Greece—Biography—Juvenile literature. 4. Greece—Kings and rulers—Biography—Juvenile literature. I. Title.
DF234.W715 2010
938'.07092—dc22
[B]

2009007423

**Tod Olson, Series Editor**
**Marie O'Neill, Art Director**
**Allicette Torres, Cover Design**
**SimonSays Design!, Book Design and Production**

© 2010 Scholastic Inc.

All rights reserved. Published by Franklin Watts, an imprint of Scholastic Inc.
Published simultaneously in Canada. Printed in the United States of America.

SCHOLASTIC, FRANKLIN WATTS, and associated logos are
trademarks and/or registered trademarks of Scholastic Inc.

11 12 13 14 15 R 19 18 17 16 15 14 13          23

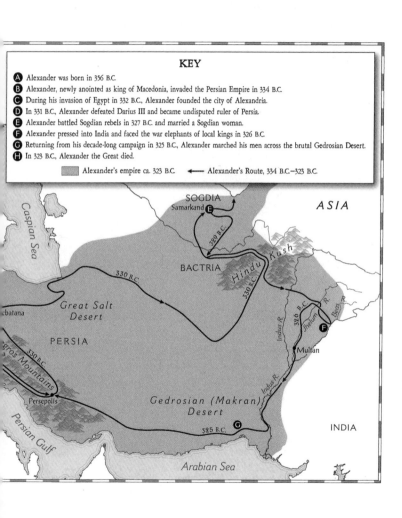

## KEY

**A** Alexander was born in 356 B.C.

**B** Alexander, newly anointed as king of Macedonia, invaded the Persian Empire in 334 B.C.

**C** During his invasion of Egypt in 332 B.C., Alexander founded the city of Alexandria.

**D** In 331 B.C., Alexander defeated Darius III and became undisputed ruler of Persia.

**E** Alexander battled Sogdian rebels in 327 B.C. and married a Sogdian woman.

**F** Alexander pressed into India and faced the war elephants of local kings in 326 B.C.

**G** Returning from his decade-long campaign in 325 B.C., Alexander marched his men across the brutal Gedrosian Desert.

**H** In 323 B.C., Alexander the Great died.

Alexander's empire ca. 323 B.C.    ⟵ Alexander's Route, 334 B.C.–323 B.C.

SOGDIA
Samarkand **E**

ASIA

Caspian Sea

329 B.C.

BACTRIA

Hindu Kush

330 B.C.

330 B.C.

Great Salt Desert

ebatana

326 B.C.

Jhelum R.

Beas R.

Indus R.

**F**

PERSIA

330 B.C.

ros Mountains

Multan

Persepolis

Indus R.

Gedrosian (Makran) Desert

325 B.C.    **G**

INDIA

Persian Gulf

Arabian Sea

# TABLE OF CONTENTS

# A Wicked Web

A look at the allies and enemies of Alexander the Great.

## Family and Friends

**KING PHILIP
OF MACEDONIA**
Alexander's father

**OLYMPIAS
OF EPIRUS**
Alexander's mother

**HEPHAESTION**
Alexander's lifelong
friend and companion

**PARMENION**
commander of
Alexander's army

**PHILOTAS**
cavalry officer and
son of Parmenion

**ALEXANDER
THE GREAT**

**ARISTOTLE**
famous Greek philosopher
and Alexander's tutor

**CLEITUS**
cavalry commander

**CALLISTHENES**
philosopher and Alexander's
official chronicler

**ROXANE**
Alexander's wife; daughter of
a Sogdian nobleman

# Enemies

**ATTALUS**
Macedonian general and
grandfather of Caranus

**CARANUS**
one of Alexander's
half brothers; a rival to
the Macedonian throne

**DARIUS III**
ruler of the Persian Empire

**BESSUS**
governor of Bactria and
general in the Persian army

**BATIS**
Persian governor of Gaza

**MEMNON**
Greek general
in the Persian army

**PORUS**
Indian king; became
an ally of Alexander

ALEXANDER THE GREAT, 356–323 B.C.

THE PEOPLE OF THE PERSIAN EMPIRE HAD never seen anything like it. For two years, an army of hardened warriors had stormed almost at will through their lands. The invaders came from the tiny kingdom of Macedonia in Europe. They had conquered the great city-states of the Greek peninsula and then carved a 1,200-mile path around the eastern shore of the Mediterranean Sea and into the heart of Asia. The foot soldiers of the invading force marched 16 deep and 16 wide, in formations known as phalanxes. Each man carried a 15-foot-long pike with razor-sharp iron tips. Bristling like gigantic porcupines, the phalanxes sliced through the ranks of the most determined defenders. With powerful catapults and battering rams, they smashed the walls of city after city.

As word of the invasion spread through the Persian Empire, the reputation of the Macedonian commander spread with it. He was Alexander, king of Macedonia and ruler of the Greek city-states. He was a master strategist on the battlefield who held the absolute loyalty of his troops. Above all, he was shockingly ambitious. He was attempting to conquer the largest empire on earth—and he had not yet celebrated his twenty-fifth birthday.

In the summer of 332 B.C., Alexander and his army reached the border of Egypt—the westernmost region in the Persian Empire. In their way stood the walled city of Gaza.

Alexander marched his men to the gates of Gaza and demanded its surrender. The governor of the city, a man named Batis, refused. Batis was convinced that he could resist Alexander. His city stood on a 250-foot-high hill surrounded by soft sand that made it difficult for an invader to move war machinery into place. To add to his defenses, Batis had hired Arab soldiers to fight off the attackers. He hoarded supplies to sustain his people in case Alexander tried to starve them out.

The supposedly invincible city was a challenge Alexander could not resist. If he seized Gaza, the feat would send a shiver of fear through the Persian Empire. Enemy governors would surely think twice before refusing an invitation to surrender.

When Alexander led his first assault on the walls, Batis's soldiers drove him back. Alexander led a second charge up the hill, but took a metal bolt in the shoulder from a Gazan catapult.

For two months, while their commander recovered, the Macedonians battled to reach the city walls. Slowly, they seized control of the high ground. They dug tunnels under the walls to weaken the foundations. They pounded at the gates with heavy battering rams.

Finally, Alexander's men broke through and stormed into the city. The Macedonian king battled hand-to-hand alongside his men in the streets. He was wounded again, this time in the leg. But before long the Gazans laid down their arms.

ALEXANDER USED 120-FOOT-TALL siege towers like this one to break into walled cities. Archers (top left) provided cover, while a bridge (center) was lowered onto the city walls. Macedonian soldiers then crossed the bridge into the city below.

Batis placed his city at Alexander's mercy—and Alexander made an example of its residents. He ordered his soldiers to kill all of Gaza's men and ship the women and children off to be sold as slaves. Then he turned his attention to Batis.

The Gazan governor, according to one account, had failed to kneel before Alexander when he finally surrendered the city. It proved to be a fatal mistake. Alexander was known to reward the courage of men who resisted his army. But to those who failed to respect him, he could be ruthless. Alexander had Batis lashed by his ankles to a chariot and dragged to his death.

Emboldened by another victory, Alexander drove his men into Egypt and beyond. His goal was nothing less than the conquest of the known world. As he came closer and closer to achieving it, he became convinced that he was descended from the gods and that no mortal could defeat him. Slowly, he appeared to descend into madness. But before his short life ended, Alexander had become the most successful conqueror in history.

# PART 1

# A Bloodstained Crown

# CHAPTER 1

# A Divine Gift

AN INVINCIBLE SON is born to an ambitious king and queen.

ON JULY 20, 356 B.C., KING PHILIP OF Macedonia was at war when he received three important messages. The king was told that his best general had won a battle, his horse had won an important race, and his wife had given birth to a son named Alexander.

"He was naturally well pleased," the ancient Greek historian Plutarch later wrote. "The fortune-tellers told him that the son whose birth was one of three successes would be invincible."

To Philip, the promise of a powerful son must have

ACCORDING TO LEGEND, the temple of Artemis burned
to the ground the night that Alexander the Great was born.
It was said that Artemis, the goddess of childbirth, chose to
stay with Alexander rather than protect her shrine.

seemed like a gift from the gods. Macedonia was a
tiny mountain kingdom with enemies on all sides and
a history of constant warfare. Its people lived in the
shadow of their sophisticated neighbors to the south,
the great city-states of Athens, Sparta, and Thebes.
These city-states—powerful, independent cities that
ruled the surrounding countryside—dominated
the Greek peninsula. The Greeks boasted brilliant
philosophers, famous playwrights, talented sculptors,

and the world's first democracies. They looked down on the Macedonians as uncultured and illiterate barbarians.

To some extent, the Greeks were right. Macedonians made their living herding sheep in the mountains or farming in the lowlands. Macedonian nobles, known as Companions, earned respect as warriors—not scholars. When they weren't on the battlefield, they spent much of their time hunting, riding horses, drinking wine, and fighting with each other.

But King Philip had bigger ambitions for his people. He invited great artists, philosophers, and engineers to the Macedonian capital of Pella. He also worked hard to transform Macedonia from a tiny feuding kingdom into a military powerhouse. Philip brought more professional soldiers into the army and trained them well. By the time Alexander was eight, his father had invaded the regions of Thrace to the east and Thessaly to the south. Philip's dream was to unite the Greeks under his rule and lead them in a great campaign against the sprawling Persian Empire to the east.

As Philip pursued his ambitions on the battlefield, Alexander grew up in a marble palace in Pella, under the protective wing of his mother, Olympias. A princess from the nearby kingdom of Epirus, Olympias was beautiful, intensely emotional, and every bit as ambitious as her husband.

Olympias was also extremely religious. She spent hours each week honoring the Greek gods in elaborate rituals. She paid frequent visits to the oracles—the priestesses who were said to use heavenly wisdom to predict events on earth. Olympias was particularly devoted to Dionysus, god of wine and revelry. She and her fellow worshippers held wild ceremonies with tame snakes and plenty of wine. They were known to sacrifice animals, dismember them, and drink their blood.

Olympias had just one obsession that rivaled her devotion to the gods: She was completely dedicated to her son and determined to make him king of Macedonia. As Philip's eldest legitimate son, Alexander stood next in line for the throne. But like most Macedonian kings before him, Philip had several wives and mistresses. If Alexander displeased his father and another wife gave birth to a son, Alexander could lose his position.

Philip must have been both proud and wary as he watched Alexander grow. A powerful son was an asset. But powerful sons could easily become threats to their fathers. And if Olympias was to be believed, this son was no ordinary mortal. She may have been responsible for a rumor that began to spread through Macedonia: Alexander's father, it was said, was not Philip but Zeus, king of the gods.

# ATHENS: CRADLE OF CIVILIZATION

DURING THE CENTURY BEFORE PHILIP CAME TO power, three cities dominated the Greek peninsula: Athens, Sparta, and Thebes. They were often at war with each other.

Despite the constant turmoil, Athens became the center of a revolution in science, the arts, and politics that gave rise to the beginnings of Western Civilization.

In the 5th century B.C., Athenian politicians created the world's first democracy. All male citizens were expected to vote on the pressing issues of the city.

Athens also produced some of history's greatest philosophers. Alexander's teacher, Aristotle, taught his students to gather evidence from nature before they formed opinions about the world. The Athenians also loved art and public performance. They filled huge outdoor arenas to watch dramas, comedies, and sporting events.

Alexander relished conquering the Athenians. But he appreciated their accomplishments enough to spread them across the world.

PHILOSOPHERS were the celebrities of Athens.

# CHAPTER 2

# Dreams of Destiny

The prince gets an education
AND MAKES AN IMPRESSION.

At age seven, Alexander began his formal education with a tutor appointed by his mother. Young Alexander may or may not have believed he was descended from the king of the gods. But he acted as though one thing were absolutely certain: He was born to be a ruler of mortals.

Alexander quickly mastered the art of warfare. He learned to handle the sharp, 15-foot Macedonian pike with ease. He rode a horse with skill and used a bow and a javelin with great accuracy. He ran so fast that he was eventually asked to compete in the gathering of athletes from all over the Greek peninsula known as the Olympic Games. "Yes," he replied, but only "if I have kings to run against me."

Alexander was just 11 or 12 when his cool self-assurance caught the eye of his father and a group of Macedonian Companions. A horse breeder had just given Philip a tall stallion called Bucephalus. The royal grooms brought the animal to a field and tried to tame him—without success. Philip angrily ordered the horse to be taken away.

Alexander spoke up boldly. "What a horse they are losing, just because they do not know the best way to handle him," he said.

Philip and the other men laughed at the young prince's nerve. But as they watched Alexander approach Bucephalus, their amusement turned to respect. Alexander had noticed that the horse was being spooked by his own shadow. Turning Bucephalus into the sun, he spoke a few soothing words. When Bucephalus

KING PHILIP SAID that no one could tame the stallion Bucephalus. But Alexander would prove his father wrong—and then ride the warhorse into countless battles over the next 20 years.

calmed down, Alexander mounted him and rode with perfect control to the end of the field and back.

The nobles burst into applause as Alexander returned. Philip wept with pride. "Son," he said, "you must find a kingdom big enough for your ambitions. Macedonia is too small to hold you."

To groom his son for such a promising future, Philip hired the best tutor he could find—the famous Greek philosopher Aristotle. Philip gave Aristotle a fine house in the quiet village of Mieza, 20 miles from Pella. When Alexander was 13, he moved to Mieza to study with the great man.

In Mieza, Alexander lived with a group of young nobles, or Companions. Many of them became friends and allies for life. His closest friend was a handsome boy named Hephaestion, who would become Alexander's lifelong friend.

Alexander grew close to Aristotle at Mieza. Under the eye of the great master, he developed a curiosity about medicine and the natural world. During his

# KING PHILIP'S ARMY

DETERMINED TO DOMINATE ALL OF GREECE, King Philip turned Macedonia's ragtag army into a disciplined, well-trained fighting force. After his early victories, he began sending prisoners of war to work the fields so that Macedonian farmers and herders could join the army full-time.

Philip's infantry quickly grew from 10,000 to 24,000. At the center of its battle line stood the Foot Companions, who marched in square phalanxes of 256 men. Their 15-foot-long lances struck opposing soldiers before the enemy could close in for hand-to-hand combat.

A regiment of elite Royal Shield Bearers protected the right flank of the Foot Companions. These were the best-trained soldiers, chosen for their size and strength.

The knockout blow, however, was usually PHALANXES SMASHED through the center of enemy lines.

CATAPULTS FIRED iron arrows over enemy walls.

made by the expert horsemen known as the Companion Cavalry, who flanked the Foot Companions on both sides. They charged on horseback, using spears and short swords to cut through enemy lines.

Philip also used a special corps of engineers who developed state-of-the-art siege towers to batter the defenses of walled cities. The engineers built wooden towers 120 feet high with platforms open to the front. The towers could be pulled next to a city's walls so that archers could fire down on the defenders.

Philip's engineers also built catapults to fling heavy iron arrows at high speeds. These devastating machines used a rope wound around a spool, or winch, to crank a firing arm into position. Alexander would eventually improve on his father's design, using twisted ropes to set the firing arm. The increased tension allowed him to hurl heavy stones as well as arrows during his march across Asia.

campaigns in Asia, he often sent samples of exotic plants and animals home to Aristotle.

Alexander also developed a love of Greek literature. He spent hours reading about the exploits of Achilles, the great Greek warrior from the well-known epic poem *The Iliad*. Aristotle gave Alexander his own treasured copy of the poem, and Alexander carried it with him for the rest of his life, often comparing himself to Achilles. Both, after all, had supposedly descended from the gods. And both had been singled out by fortune-tellers for a life of glory.

In 340 B.C., Alexander's education came to an abrupt end. King Philip was planning a military campaign, and he needed someone to rule in his absence. He decided that his son was ready for the task.

At Philip's command, Alexander returned to Pella to become regent of Macedonia. He was just 16 years old—and this was his chance to prove that, like Achilles, he was destined for great things.

# CHAPTER 3

# The Family That Fights Together . . .

Alexander and his father
go to war against the
GREAT CITIES OF GREECE.

ALEXANDER HAD BARELY RETURNED TO
Pella when he met his first big test. Border tribes in
Thrace, to the northeast, rebelled and threatened to
cut off trade routes in and out of Pella.

Alexander mounted Bucephalus, the wild horse
he had tamed, and led his warriors into battle. He
seized the city at the center of the rebellion, expelled

its inhabitants, and replaced them with Greek settlers loyal to Macedonia. Then, as if to announce to the world the scale of his ambitions, he renamed the city Alexandropolis.

Alexander's first campaign had ended in a rousing success. Philip returned to Pella and rewarded his son by making him a general.

Father and son spent the next two years fighting side by side. They led the powerful Macedonian phalanxes through Thrace, bringing the region under control. During one battle, Philip fell wounded on the field. Alexander supposedly stood over him with a shield and beat off the attackers with his sword.

In the summer of 339 B.C., Philip and Alexander made a final assault on the city-states of the Greek peninsula. They swept southward with 2,000 cavalry and 30,000 foot soldiers. Within a year, they fought their way to a town called Chaeronea, just north of Thebes. There, they found a combined force from Athens and Thebes waiting for them.

ALEXANDER COMMANDED his first army when he was just 16.
Here, his phalanxes annihilate a rebellious tribe from Thrace.

At dawn on August 4, 338 B.C., the two sides met on a battlefield to decide the future of the Greek peninsula. Philip commanded the phalanxes on the right wing of the Macedonian army. He put Alexander in charge of the cavalry to the left.

Philip's phalanxes leveled their lances and charged. The Macedonian battle cry—*Alalalalalai*—rang out over the clash of swords and shields. Philip momentarily retreated, drawing the Athenians forward. Alexander's cavalry dashed into a gap between the Thebans and the

Athenians. His charge shattered the Greek lines. The Athenians broke ranks and ran, while the Thebans fought to the death. In the end, the Macedonians killed at least 1,000 Greeks and captured another 2,000.

Philip had been fighting for two decades to see this day. The entire Greek peninsula lay within his grasp. The following month, he gathered Greek leaders together and had them name him Supreme Commander of Greek Forces.

Now in control of all the Greek city-states, Philip returned home to Pella with his son. With the armies of Greece at his command, he began to lay plans for the invasion of the Persian Empire.

# Murder!

## Alexander takes over after his
## FATHER'S MYSTERIOUS DEATH.

DESPITE THEIR SUCCESSES TOGETHER ON the battlefield, Philip and Alexander turned on each other when they returned to Pella. In 337 B.C., Philip made a move that infuriated his son. He married a woman named Eurydice, the young niece of Attalus, an important military officer. The king's latest wife posed a serious danger to Olympias and her son. Unlike Olympias, Eurydice was a native-born Macedonian. Any son of hers would be a full-blooded

Macedonian prince and might have a better chance at becoming king than Alexander.

Family tensions erupted into conflict at the wedding banquet. Attalus spent the night drinking glass after glass of wine. When he finally stood to make a toast, he congratulated the newlyweds. Then he told everyone to pray that his niece might soon produce a "legitimate heir" to the Macedonian throne.

According to one account, Alexander shot to his feet. "Are you calling me a bastard?" he yelled and threw his cup of wine at Attalus.

Furious at his son's outburst, Philip got up and drew his sword, but he was so drunk that he fell over before he could attack Alexander. "This is the man who wants to invade Asia," Alexander scoffed, "but he can't even make it from his couch to mine!"

Alexander stormed from the room, knowing that his father would not soon forgive the insult. He gathered his close friends and his mother and fled the country.

The group spent a year in exile before Philip sent a

family friend to negotiate a truce. But when Alexander came home, his position was no more secure than before. In the spring of 336 B.C., Philip sent an advance force into the Persian Empire and gave Attalus a high command. Alexander stayed home in Pella, where Eurydice soon gave birth to a son. Philip named the son Caranus, after the founder of the royal dynasty—not a good sign for Alexander's future.

That summer, Philip's family gathered at an arena just south of Pella for a celebration. The king stood at the height of his power. He ruled all of Greece. He was about to launch his campaign against Persia. He had a new son. And now, his daughter—Alexander's sister, Cleopatra—was about to marry a neighboring king.

A long procession filed into the arena as the celebration began. A line of statues representing Greek gods were rolled in on carts. Alexander came next. Then, as Philip prepared to make his grand entrance, the captain of the royal bodyguard approached the king, drew a short sword, and drove it between his ribs.

KING PHILIP IS STABBED in the chest by his own bodyguard, clearing the way for Alexander to become king. People whispered that Alexander was to blame for his father's murder.

Philip died instantly. Three bodyguards chased down the assassin and killed him before he revealed any information about who had planned the murder.

With a single act of violence, Alexander's time had come. Fearing rebellion in Philip's newly conquered lands, the nobles of Macedonia needed a new king who would take over immediately and rule with a strong hand. They rejected the infant Caranus in favor of Alexander. At the age of 20, the young warrior had become a king.

# CHAPTER 5

# In Command

### As a sign of things to come, Alexander SHOWS THE GREEKS WHO'S BOSS.

As THE NEW KING OF MACEDONIA, Alexander immediately took steps to seize a firm hold on power. To silence the rumors that he and Olympias had planned Philip's murder, he led an inquiry into the assassination—which conveniently blamed nearly all of his enemies for the crime. One by one, the new king's rivals for the throne were accused of treason and executed. Attalus was killed on the way back from the Persian Empire. Alexander's

ALEXANDER AND HIS MOTHER, Queen Olympias (left), had dozens of their rivals killed after King Philip's assassination.

half brothers were rounded up and executed. Even Eurydice's tiny son, Caranus, was killed.

Olympias herself took care of Eurydice. A story was widely told at the time that she roasted Philip's younger wife alive over hot coals.

After wiping out his enemies at home, Alexander turned his attention to neighboring kingdoms that had begun to rise up against him. He swept east and north to the Danube River, subduing the rebellious tribes of Thrace. Then he turned to Athens and Thebes, whose leaders were planning a revolt.

In just 13 days, Alexander marched his battle-weary army 250 miles to the gates of Thebes. He blocked the city's escape routes and rolled his siege towers and catapults up to its walls. When the Thebans spurned an invitation to surrender, the Macedonians broke through the walls and overwhelmed the city's defenders.

Then Alexander gave an order that he knew would send a clear message to every city in Greece. He told his men to kill every Theban fighter they could capture and imprison all other citizens. In all, the Macedonians slaughtered 6,000 Thebans and sold another 20,000 as slaves. Then they burned the ancient city completely to the ground.

In a grand gesture, Alexander spared Athens. But the people of Greece had gotten the message. All the Greek leaders swore allegiance to the new Macedonian king. The stage was set for the campaign that Alexander's father had dreamed about for years—the invasion of the Persian Empire.

# PART 2

Into the East

# CHAPTER 6

# Invasion!

## The conqueror
## HURLS THE FIRST SPEAR.

On a may morning in 334 b.c., Alexander stood at the front of his flagship wearing full armor and gripping a spear. Behind him trailed a fleet of ships packed with more than 40,000 soldiers and 5,000 swift horses. With them were dozens of engineers, shipbuilders, doctors, and scholars. The retinue also included Aristotle's nephew, a philosopher named Callisthenes, whose job was to record the great conquests that Alexander expected to achieve.

The fleet crossed slowly from Europe into Asia over

a narrow, saltwater strait called the Hellespont (known today as the Dardanelles). Alexander's boat landed on the shore of Phrygia, a province at the northwestern edge of the Persian Empire (in present-day Turkey). Alexander flung his spear into the sand and claimed the entire Persian Empire as his own. The invasion had finally begun.

Alexander's men must have marveled at the task that lay ahead of them. The Persian Empire stretched for 4,000 miles, from the deserts of Egypt in the west to the Indus River in the east (in present-day Pakistan).

The Greeks regarded the Persians, their great enemies, as barbarians. The Persians had seized Greek colonies in western Asia and twice invaded the Greek peninsula. In 480 B.C., a Persian army had set fire to Athens. Greek warriors pushed them back across the Hellespont, but Persian kings still ruled thousands of Greek settlers in western Asia.

Alexander wanted revenge for the destruction of Athens, and he had promised the Greek soldiers who had joined his army that he would liberate all the Greeks in the Persian Empire.

But Alexander also admired the Persian rulers. Fanning out from the Persian homeland (in present-day Iran), their armies had conquered some 45 separate nations with a combined population of many millions.

To rule such a diverse empire, Persia's kings had to be tolerant and smart. In each domain they conquered, they replaced the local king with a loyal governor, known as a satrap. The satrap collected taxes to send to Persia, but otherwise left local governments—known as satrapies—intact.

When Alexander landed in Asia, the Persian king of kings, Darius III, had only recently come to power. At six and a half feet tall, Darius towered over the priests, advisers, and admirers who surrounded him. As a young warrior, he had earned a reputation for bravery. Now he lived in tremendous luxury in Persepolis, the home of the great Persian kings. Thanks to a steady income of silver and gold from his satraps, he was the richest man in the world. Persian priests taught that he was god's representative on earth.

Alexander was not intimidated by the Persian ruler's reputation. After landing on Persian soil, the Macedonian leader went directly to the ruins of Troy, where his hero Achilles had supposedly been killed. Alexander and his friend Hephaestion raced around Achilles' tomb. They visited a temple where a shield said to have belonged to Achilles hung on the wall. Alexander took the shield and vowed to carry it with him into battle.

DARIUS III RULED over the Persian Empire, the richest and largest empire in the world. Twice the Persians had almost conquered the city-states of Greece.

ALEXANDER AND HIS MEN EXPLORE the tomb of Achilles amidst the ruins of Troy. Achilles was the greatest hero of Greek legend, and Alexander hoped to surpass his glory.

He would soon get a chance to test the shield's strength. Across the Granicus River, less than 100 miles away, a Persian force had gathered to defend the empire. And they were eager to fight.

# CHAPTER 7

# First Blood

## THE ARMIES OF TWO EMPIRES CLASH on the banks of the Granicus River.

ALEXANDER MOVED EAST TOWARD HIS first great battle with the armies of Persia. He arrived at the Granicus River on a May evening in 334 B.C. Arrayed along the steep bank across the river was Darius's army. The Persian ruler had confidently stayed in Persepolis and left the command to his satraps, who fielded a force of about 10,000 cavalry and 15,000 infantry. The army included several thousand

Greek mercenaries, commanded by a Greek general named Memnon.

Alexander stood on the riverbank, distinguished from his men by two tall white plumes of horsehair streaming from his helmet. His top commander, Parmenion, had led many attacks as Philip's most trusted general. Now Parmenion approached Alexander and advised him to wait until dawn to make the dangerous river crossing. Alexander insisted that the time to strike was now.

"There was a profound hush as both armies stood for a while motionless on the brink of the river, as if in awe of what was to come," writes the ancient Greek historian Arrian. It was the last moment of stillness before a war that would change the history of the world.

Then came a blast of trumpets and the terrorizing *Alalalalai!* of the Macedonian battle cry.

According to one account of the battle, Alexander led the Companion Cavalry charging headlong across the river. The horses bogged down in the mud on the

ALEXANDER'S INVASION of Persia began with his charge across the Granicus River. Alexander (with white-plumed helmet) was struck in the head with an ax during the battle.

far bank. Their riders were forced to dismount and fight the Persians hand-to-hand.

In the chaos of clashing swords, two Persian officers spotted the white plumes of Alexander's helmet. They rushed at the Macedonian king. While Alexander fought with one, the other swung his battle ax down on the king's head. The blow split Alexander's helmet, and the blade grazed his hair. As the Persian officer raised his ax to strike again, a Macedonian soldier named

Cleitus ran him through with his spear. Saved from certain death, Alexander recovered and killed the other Persian officer with his sword.

By this time, the phalanxes of the Macedonian Foot Companions had crossed the river and linked up with Alexander. With Parmenion commanding the left flank and his son Philotas the right, they fought their way up the riverbank. Alexander's cavalrymen freed their horses from the mud, remounted, and charged at the Persian army. On equal ground at last, the Macedonians shattered the enemy lines. The Persians broke ranks and fled.

Alexander let the Persians go but ordered his men to surround the Greek mercenaries. To Alexander, they were traitors who deserved no mercy. In the midst of a furious assault, the Greek commander, Memnon, escaped. His soldiers were not so lucky. Most of them were killed in battle. The 2,000 who survived were sent off in chains to the silver mines of Macedonia.

Alexander had announced his arrival.

# CHAPTER 8

༼ས༼ས༼ས༼ས༼ས༼ས༼ས༼ས

# War Games

### Alexander advances, as Darius scrambles to prepare AN ARMY WORTHY OF THE CHALLENGE.

AFTER HIS VICTORY AT GRANICUS, Alexander turned south and moved slowly down the coast, surveying his strategic position. The Persian navy boasted twice as many warships as the Macedonians could muster. To offset his disadvantage at sea, Alexander decided to rely on his strength—his land army. He would seize all the port cities on the coast and strangle the Persian navy by leaving its ships no place to dock and resupply.

City after city fell before the Macedonian advance. Sardis, Ephesus, and Priene, with their large Greek populations, welcomed Alexander as a liberator. Miletus and Halicarnassus resisted, but gave in under pressure from the Macedonian catapults and battering rams.

In most places, Alexander took steps to win the loyalty of the people. He installed Macedonian rulers but freed conquered cities from taxes and left their local laws intact. He also stopped treating Greek

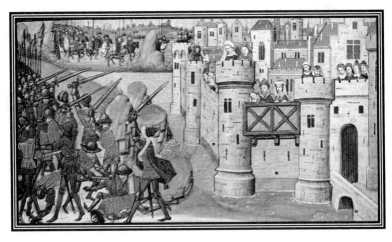

ALEXANDER HAD VOWED to liberate the Greeks in the Persian Empire. Here, the Greeks of Ephesus watch as Alexander's army slaughters the city's Persian leaders.

mercenaries as traitors and welcomed them into his army.

In the fall of 334 B.C., Alexander halted his march down the coast, having neutralized the Persian navy. He disbanded his own navy, saving only 20 ships to carry siege towers down the coast. He sent his married soldiers home for the winter, and then moved north to complete his conquest of Phrygia before Darius could raise another large army.

Several weeks' march to the southeast, Darius had taken up residence in the Persian capital of Babylon to prepare the defense of his empire. Each week, new recruits streamed in from the farthest reaches of the empire. Darius spent vast quantities of gold and silver to equip them with gleaming armor, shields, battle axes, lances, and swords. With thousands of mounted cavalry and row after row of well-armed infantry, the emperor's army made an impressive display.

Darius was ready to take command of this imposing force himself, and most of his advisers flattered him into thinking he could not lose. But one man, an Athenian mercenary named Charidemus, dared to challenge Darius. The Persian troops, in all their finery, he said, were no match for Alexander's battle-hardened men.

"The Macedonian line is coarse and inelegant," Charidemus warned, but they were disciplined, accustomed to hardship, and fiercely loyal to their leader. "What you need is strength like theirs," he added. "Send off that silver and gold of yours and hire *soldiers*."

Darius flew into a rage. He ordered his guards to seize the brash Athenian and kill him. As he was being led to his death, Charidemus refused to be silenced. He called out for all to hear that Darius had become drunk with power and forgotten his common sense. "You will pay the penalty for rejecting my advice!" Charidemus said. He was still shouting when his throat was cut.

# CHAPTER 9

# The Battle of Issus

Darius and Alexander meet
on the battlefield—AND THE
PERSIAN KING BLINKS.

IN THE SUMMER OF 333 B.C., AS DARIUS
readied his soldiers, Alexander completed his conquest
of Phrygia's cities. He welcomed fresh troops from
Greece and then led his reinforced army back to the
Mediterranean coast. The men marched through a
pass in the Taurus Mountains called the Cilician Gates
and entered a narrow plain between the mountains
and the Bay of Issus. Alexander hoped to lure Darius
into the cramped battlefield, where the Persians

would be unable to use their superior numbers to their advantage.

In the fall, Alexander got his wish. Darius arrived at the Bay of Issus in a tall chariot glistening with gold and gems. Surrounding him was a vast army, perhaps as large as 100,000 men. The Persian fighters outnumbered Alexander's men by about three to one.

When the two armies had formed their lines and readied for battle, Alexander rode out and spoke to his soldiers. According to the historian Curtius, the Macedonian king praised his men for their bravery and reminded them of the burning of Athens by the Persians 150 years before. Now they had a chance to take revenge, he told them. If they succeeded, they would be in a position "to subdue not only the Persians but all the races of the earth."

Surveying the battlefield, Alexander saw that the strong Persian cavalry stood to his left, across the Payas River. To the right, he noticed a weakness in the Persian line. A battalion of infantry stationed against a hill was protected by a company of archers. Guessing that the infantry were new and untrained, Alexander mounted Bucephalus and charged to the right, galloping across the river at the head of the Companion Cavalry.

Despite their vast advantage in numbers, the Persians quickly collapsed. The archers loosed their arrows into the Macedonian onslaught and then turned and ran, causing chaos among the Persian infantry as they fled.

Alexander and his horsemen broke through the crumbling Persian line and charged at Darius, who towered above his army in his chariot. Alexander was wounded by a sword-blow to his leg, but he pressed on toward the Persian king.

As the Macedonians closed in, Darius jumped onto a horse and fled for Babylon. He left behind a devastated army, still fighting into the night.

The mighty Persian ruler had also deserted his own family. Behind the Persian lines that night, Alexander's men found the royal tent, occupied by Darius's mother, one of his wives, his infant son, and two of his daughters.

Alexander received them graciously and promised that they would be treated like royalty.

Then Alexander entered the emperor's sumptuous tent, with its carpets, wooden furniture, and bathtub. Accustomed to the more modest surroundings of Macedonian royalty, Alexander was dazzled. "When

RIDING HIS WAR-HORSE Bucephalus, Alexander hacks his way toward Darius during the Battle of Issus. After the Macedonians broke through the Persian lines, the battle quickly became a terrible slaughter.

he saw the jars and pitchers and tubs and boxes, all of gold and intricately wrought, and smelled the delicious fragrance of spices and perfumes," says Plutarch, "he looked at his friends and said, 'This, it seems, is to be a king.'"

C H A P T E R   1 0

# Crucifying Tyre

## At a famed stronghold, defenders PAY HORRIBLY FOR RESISTING THE KING.

AT THE CLOSE OF 333 B.C., ALEXANDER had been in Asia just a year and a half. His victories had filled him with confidence. All of Anatolia (present-day Turkey) was securely in his control. He had met the Persian ruler face-to-face and defeated him. Darius's own family owed their survival to Alexander's mercy. It was enough to make a young king swell with pride.

ALEXANDER PROMISES MERCY to Darius's family.
The Persian emperor had abandoned them while fleeing
the carnage at the Battle of Issus.

Now Alexander set his sights southward, toward the fabled kingdom of Egypt, with its vast stores of grain and its strategic position on the Mediterranean Sea.

Once again, he moved down the Mediterranean coast, seizing port cities to isolate the Persian navy. In January 332 B.C., he reached a major prize, the seaport city of Tyre. The city stood behind high walls on an island 900 yards offshore. This was the stronghold of the Phoenicians, a powerful seafaring people who provided most of Darius's navy.

When Alexander and his men arrived outside Tyre, he met with the city's leaders and demanded that they surrender.

They refused, and Alexander almost went mad with anger. He did not have the naval strength to assault the island city by sea. But he was determined to destroy the Tyrians—even if he had to move the earth to do it.

Alexander decided to build a land bridge to Tyre. Undaunted by the sheer size of the task, he rounded up thousands of local villagers for forced labor. He sent some of them to demolish the walls of an old city for stone. The rest were marched off to collect timber in a nearby forest.

Stone by stone, plank by plank, the land bridge began to take shape. When the Tyrian navy attacked by sea, Alexander had his men widen the bridge. Then they rolled 120-foot-tall siege towers onto it and rained arrows and stones down on the attacking warships.

The tide began to turn in Alexander's favor when warships arrived from Cyprus, an island nation that had rebelled against Persian rule. The Cypriot navy fought off the Tyrian warships and weakened the walls of Tyre with seaborne battering rams.

ALEXANDER ALLIED with nearby Cyprus, and its navy attacked the island fortress of Tyre. When the city finally fell, Alexander had 2,000 of its people crucified and another 30,000 enslaved.

When the bridge reached the island, Alexander sent wave after wave of men at the city walls. The Tyrians poured sand laced with burning sulfur down on the attackers, sending them screaming in agony into the water to drown.

Finally, Alexander himself climbed a siege tower and led the Macedonians over the wall. It was July, and the king had wasted seven months on the siege. His obsession with Tyre had led him to risk almost everything on its conquest.

Alexander took out his anger on the Tyrians, sending 30,000 of them into slavery in chains. According to one account, he nailed 2,000 men to crosses and left them to die on the shore.

# CHAPTER 11

# Oracle in the Desert

Alexander takes a detour
in Egypt to RECEIVE A MESSAGE
FROM THE GODS.

Having defeated the defenders of Tyre, Alexander marched west toward Egypt. He besieged Gaza and executed its governor in gruesome fashion. Then he entered the oldest civilization in the Mediterranean world. "Compared to us, you Greeks are just children," Egyptian priests had once told a Greek visitor.

ALEXANDER'S ARMY STANDS before the Great Sphinx, which was already two thousand years old. The Egyptians had suffered under Persian rule, and they eagerly named Alexander their pharaoh.

Alexander led his men into the sacred city of Heliopolis, famed for its white walls and red granite obelisk. He marched them past the pyramids of Giza, which gleamed with polished white limestone.

The people of Egypt welcomed Alexander. For two centuries they had been ruled by Persian satraps, who taxed the people heavily and insulted their ancient traditions. Alexander, by contrast, offered sacrifices to the Egyptian gods. In the city of Memphis, Egypt's high priests offered him the ancient title of pharaoh, or king, which he proudly accepted.

With Egypt in his possession, Alexander went on a risky spiritual quest. In January 331 B.C., with a small guard and a few local guides, he set out across the Sahara Desert, west of the Nile River. His goal was the sacred oasis of Siwa, home to the oracle of Amun, king of the Egyptian gods.

Alexander was desperate to consult Amun, whom he associated with the Greek god Zeus. "He . . . had

ALEXANDER MEETS with the priests of the god Amun.
Alexander believed that Amun was the Egyptians' name
for Zeus, king of the Greek gods. The priests may have
told Alexander that Zeus was his true father.

a feeling," writes Arrian, "that in some way he was
descended from Amun."

The desert march lasted eight long days. When he
and his men finally reached Siwa, Alexander was struck
by the beauty of the oasis. A wide, deeply green plain
stretched for more than 60 miles. Orchards of olive,
lemon, pomegranate, and fig trees covered the travelers

in cool shade. At the heart of the oasis rose a giant rock with a mud-brick fortress perched on top. Inside the fortress was the temple of the oracle.

Alexander climbed to the temple, where he was greeted by the high priest of Siwa. The conqueror was then led alone into the inner chamber, so he could pose his questions directly to Amun. Unknown to its visitors, the chamber had a false ceiling. Above it, a priest hid to listen to the queries of visitors. Then another priest delivered a written response, supposedly from the god.

No one knows exactly what Alexander asked, but it's likely that he had one burning question on his mind: Was he, as his mother believed, descended from the king of the gods?

According to Arrian, Alexander received "the answer which his heart desired." From this point on, it was said, he believed that he was a god come to life on earth.

# CITY ON THE SEA

WHILE IN EGYPT, ALEXANDER FOUNDED ONE of the most impressive monuments to his success: the city of Alexandria. Located at the mouth of the Nile Delta, it was one of nearly 70 cities founded by Alexander—30 of which bore his name.

The king paid special attention to this Alexandria, which he intended to be a crossroads for travelers between Europe, Africa, and Asia. He paced out its outline, positioned the marketplace and the temples, and helped design the royal palace.

The city became an international meeting place. Merchants from Europe, Arabia, and India gathered in its streets. It was governed by Macedonians and peopled

by Greeks, Egyptians, and Jews. In 100 years, Alexandria became the largest city on earth.

THE KING MAPS OUT the city of Alexandria.

# CHAPTER 12

# Final Showdown

Alexander spurns a peace offering
from Darius and presses on to
THE ULTIMATE BATTLE.

NEWS OF THE FALL OF EGYPT TRAVELED
east to Darius. The Persian ruler had retreated to the
capital city of Babylon after his defeat at the Bay of Issus.
From his lavish palace, Darius sent off a messenger to
Alexander's camp bearing a plea to end the fighting.
In return for peace, he offered half his empire, his
daughter's hand in marriage, and a large sum of money.

The messenger arrived in 331 B.C., as Alexander
marched east out of Egypt in search of Darius.

Alexander sent the man back with a scornful reply. Darius, he insisted, must call him "Lord of Asia." "Everything you possess is now mine . . . " he went on. "Wherever you may hide yourself, be sure I shall seek you out."

Darius knew he would have to face the Macedonian king again, so he turned to the distant plain of Bactria (in present-day Afghanistan) for help. Bactria's native horsemen were as hardy and fierce as the Macedonians. Their satrap was a power-hungry chieftain named Bessus. Darius didn't trust Bessus, but he needed the Bactrian's warriors. He sent word to Bessus, asking him to raise the largest army he could and march to the aid of Babylon.

Once again, nearly 100,000 soldiers gathered in Babylon from lands far and wide. The force outnumbered Alexander's by two to one. The Persian cavalry held a three-to-one advantage over the Macedonians. Persian horsemen also fielded 200 armed chariots with spears bristling off the front and sharp blades extending from the wheels.

The two armies came together on a level plain near the small town of Gaugamela (in present-day Iraq). The weather was hot and dry. Clouds of dust rose as the generals positioned their battalions across a front that was three miles wide.

On October 1, 331 B.C., the kings and their armies began the climactic battle of the war. Bessus and his cavalry hit first, on Alexander's right. Their armed chariots terrified Alexander's men, who broke in disarray. Persian horsemen poured through the line.

The rest of the Persian cavalry swung to the left of Alexander's lines and encircled his army. Now Alexander had real trouble. The Persian chariots were thundering through his phalanxes; the enemy cavalry was already in his rear. Thinking the battle won, the Persians began to plunder the Macedonian supplies.

But amid the dusty mayhem, Alexander saw a chance. A gap had opened in the Persian center as more horsemen joined the rush around the Macedonian

lines. Alexander quickly formed his cavalry and his
infantry into a wedge. He drove it straight through
the gap—right at Darius and his bodyguards.

The bloodshed was gruesome. Men slashed and
stabbed at each other with axes, swords, and spears.

PERSIAN WAR CHARIOTS on the attack during the Battle of Gaugamela. The Persians encircled the Macedonian army and nearly destroyed it, but Alexander led a breakout aimed directly at Darius.

"The ground was littered with the severed limbs of soldiers," says the historian Curtius.

Darius, sensing that the battle was lost, turned his chariot around and fled.

On the dust-choked plain of Gaugamela, the last of the great Persian rulers had been defeated. His vast empire passed into the hands of the Macedonian invader. For Alexander, the way to the great Persian cities and all their riches lay wide open.

## BORN OF THE GODS?

The same day Alexander was born the temple of Artemis burned. Some said that Artemis, the goddess of childbirth, decided to stay with Alexander rather than protect her shrine.

## BUCEPHALUS

At age 12, Alexander won his father's respect by training the wild stallion Bucephalus. The horse accompanied Alexander into battle for the next 20 years.

## HIGHER LEARNING

Aristotle was the greatest philosopher of the age. In 343 B.C., he became Alexander's tutor.

## ACHILLES THE GREAT

Alexander often compared himself to Achilles (right), the legendary Greek warrior.

## THE KING IS DEAD

After his father was assassinated in 336 B.C., Alexander used the murder as an excuse to kill all of his political rivals.

## PERSIAN EMPEROR

Alexander planned to take over the vast empire of Darius III (left).

## TOP RECRUITS

For his army, Alexander recruited skilled soldiers from outside Macedonia—including Greek hoplites (right), the best foot soldiers in the world.

## INVASION!

In 334 B.C., Alexander invaded the Persian Empire and routed a 25,000-man army at Granicus.

## GEARS OF WAR

Alexander used catapults (left) to knock down fortress walls, and siege engines (page 14) to climb over them. Catapults were also used on the battlefield to scatter enemy troops.

## GORDIAN KNOT

In 333 B.C., Alexander wintered in Gordium. According to legend, the person who untied the famous knot there—the Gordian knot—would conquer all of Asia. Alexander hacked it apart with his sword.

## ROYAL WELCOME

After winning the Battle of Issus, Alexander moved west into Egypt. He was given the ancient title of pharaoh and proclaimed a descendant of the gods.

## FORGING BONDS

Alexander encouraged his men to marry locals to knit together the diverse people of his empire.

## PERSEPOLIS RUINED

In 330 B.C., Alexander sacked the Persian capital of Persepolis and burned the Palace of Xerxes (ruins at left) to the ground.

## END OF AN EMPEROR

After hunting Darius III for months, Alexander finally found him—but the Persian emperor had already been fatally stabbed.

## FIT FOR A KING

After conquering Persepolis, Alexander began to adopt the clothing and customs of a Persian emperor.

## AN UGLY CRIME

After a night of heavy drinking, Alexander murdered his old friend Cleitus. Alexander was growing paranoid and unstable.

## A WORTHY RIVAL

King Porus of India astride his war elephant. Porus and Alexander became allies after fighting a fierce battle on the banks of the Jhelum River in India.

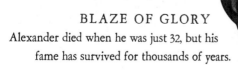

## BLAZE OF GLORY

Alexander died when he was just 32, but his fame has survived for thousands of years.

# PART 3

# Lord of Asia

~~~~~~~~~~~~~~~~~~~~~~~~

# CHAPTER 13

# Treasures of Babylon

## Asia's new ruler SEIZES A VAST HOARD OF RICHES.

WITH DARIUS FINALLY VANQUISHED, the people of Babylon threw open their gates and welcomed Alexander. The new king of kings made an emperor's entry into the capital of the Persian Empire. Perched high on a chariot, he rode through the Ishtar Gate, a giant entryway that glittered with brilliant blue mosaics. Next came his most loyal officers, the dashing aristocrats of the Companion Cavalry. As children,

ALEXANDER MAKES a triumphant entrance into Babylon, one of the two great capitals of the Persian Empire. Later, he conquered Persepolis, the ceremonial capital of the empire.

many of them had studied alongside Alexander, absorbing the wisdom of the great Aristotle. Now they shared in their friend and leader's triumph. Several bore wounds from Granicus and other battles. Alexander's dearest friend, Hephaestion, had been stabbed in the arm with a spear.

The conquerors rode through the city along avenues carpeted with flowers. Silver altars by the roadside brimmed with frankincense and other perfumes. The city's leaders lavished gifts on the Macedonians: herds of cattle and horses; cages full of lions, leopards, and other exotic animals.

In 331 B.C., Babylon was probably the world's most populous city, with nearly 200,000 residents. The city boasted hundreds of temples and palaces. It also had a reputation for wild parties. "The moral corruption there is unparalleled," wrote the Roman historian Curtius. "The Babylonians are especially addicted to wine and the excesses that go along with drunkenness. Women attend dinner parties."

Babylon had been occupied for 200 years by the Persians, who largely ignored local religious customs. As he had done in Egypt, Alexander won the approval of the residents by going immediately to the city's central temple. Taking instruction from the Babylonian priests, he made sacrifices to their god Bel.

Alexander then settled into the lavish 600-room palace of the ancient king Nebuchadnezzar. There, he attended to the business of governing his ever-growing empire. He met with advisers and local officials. He sent orders to the long list of satraps he had installed to govern his conquests. From the city's royal treasury, he paid bonuses to his soldiers.

After five weeks of rest, Alexander gathered his army and marched east. Still ahead lay the ultimate prize: Persepolis, the dazzling city at the heart of Persia. Along the way, Alexander stopped at the city of Susa. There, in one of Darius's many palaces, he found a stash of treasures from the Persians' invasion of Greece in 480 B.C. He took care to send two bronze statues of Greek heroes back to Athens.

In early 330 B.C., Alexander approached Persepolis, where he encountered tough resistance. He was ambushed at a narrow pass outside the city and suffered heavy casualties before breaking through.

AFTER PERSEPOLIS FELL to Alexander, the city was looted and thousands of its people were sold into slavery. Here, Alexander and his men prepare to burn the Palace of Xerxes.

When Alexander finally reached the gates of Persepolis, the city's military commander surrendered without a fight. But the city priests refused to honor the Macedonian with the ceremonial title of Great King. Alexander retaliated by allowing his men to loot the city. They stayed until spring, seizing a pile of silver and gold so large that it amounted to 300 times the annual income of Athens. Alexander needed 7,000 pack animals to carry the treasure away.

The Persian Empire and all its wealth now rested in Alexander's hands. His weary soldiers might have thought they would finally get to return home. But their king was far from finished. To the east lay vast reaches of uncharted land. Darius was still out there somewhere, on the run.

In June, Alexander set off on the Persian king's trail. Before he left, during a night of drunken revelry, the king and some of his men lit torches and burned the stunning Palace of Xerxes to the ground.

# CHAPTER 14

# An Emperor Abandoned

After his enemy is
stabbed and left to die,
ALEXANDER VOWS REVENGE.

SETTING OFF FROM THE CITY OF PERSEPOLIS, Alexander drove his men hard. They crossed the deadly Great Salt Desert in just 11 days. In less than a month, they caught up with Darius near the Caspian Sea, 500 miles north of Persepolis.

Alexander's men were shocked by what they found. The great king of Persia lay tied up in the back of a wagon, fatally stabbed by Bessus's Bactrian guards. After betraying his former ally, Bessus had declared himself the true ruler of the Persian Empire and fled into Bactria.

Alexander was horrified to learn of his rival's fate. Kings could be overcome in battle, he believed,

ALEXANDER KNEELS before Darius III. The Persian emperor had fled east after the Battle of Gaugamela. He was then murdered by his satrap Bessus, who declared himself the new emperor of Persia.

but they should always be honored as kings. He sent Darius's body back to Persepolis for a royal burial. Then he led his men east to hunt the traitor Bessus.

As Alexander marched his army deep into the east, his men began to notice a change in their beloved king. More and more he began to adopt the traditions of his Persian predecessors. Traditionally, the king of Persia commanded great deference. When he traveled, attendants followed him with parasols to block the sun and whisks to keep flies away. Nobles who dined with the king saved food from their table as a gift to the ruler. All subjects were expected to kneel in his presence.

When Alexander became Lord of Asia, his Persian subjects treated him according to tradition. By some accounts, Alexander grew to enjoy his new privileges, and some Macedonians believed he had become drunk on the absolute power of a Persian king.

In 330 B.C., the first rift opened in Alexander's inner circle. Alexander owed a great debt to Philotas, a leader

ALEXANDER ENTERTAINS a local nobleman at his
Persian-style court. Alexander (seated top left) had begun to dress
in the style of a Persian king, which offended many of his men.

of the Companion Cavalry, and his father, Parmenion,
the top general in the Macedonian army. But Philotas
had been critical of Alexander for some time. He
publicly scorned Alexander's claim to be descended

from Zeus. Philotas also boasted that he and his father were responsible for Alexander's great military victories.

In the fall, Alexander decided to silence the criticism once and for all. He accused Philotas of conspiring to murder him. Philotas insisted he was innocent, but Hephaestion and other Companions testified against him. Eventually, he confessed under torture. Alexander had Philotas stoned to death for treason.

Alexander then laid a trap for Parmenion. He sent a forged message under guard to the old general, who had been put in charge of a satrapy in the Zagros Mountains, 800 miles to the west. The message, supposedly from Philotas, informed Parmenion that the plot had succeeded and Alexander was dead. The general supposedly smiled at the news, at which point Alexander's men killed him on the spot.

With these ruthless acts, the Lord of Asia had squandered the two men who had made his conquest possible.

# CHAPTER 15

# Rebels Everywhere

## Alexander fights to KEEP HIS SUBJECTS IN LINE.

IN THE SPRING OF 329 B.C., ALEXANDER trailed Bessus through the snowy Hindu Kush mountains, across the wide-open plains of Bactria, and into the kingdom of Sogdia at the northernmost fringe of the Persian Empire. Tired of running, the Bactrian cavalry abandoned Bessus. Alexander captured him and sent him to be tried by a Persian court for the murder of Darius. For his crime, the traitor had his nose and ears cut off before being led to a public execution.

THE SATRAP BESSUS meets his painful end. Just as he had betrayed Darius III, the pretender was betrayed by his own troops.

With his rival out of the way, Alexander settled into the Sogdian capital of Samarkand. Using the city as a base, he spent the next year and a half battling the fiercely independent tribes of Sogdia and Bactria.

As the fighting wore on, tempers flared among the Macedonians. Alexander and many of his men had been away from home for six years. They had traveled thousands of miles, fighting their way through unfamiliar territory. Every Macedonian had watched friends die in battle. They were adrift in a land whose people were sometimes friendly and sometimes hostile. Everyone they encountered dressed strangely, spoke strange languages, and ate strange food.

The farther east they traveled, the more their king seemed to embrace the foreign customs. Alexander dressed like a Persian king. He surrounded himself with Persian slaves and attendants. To many of his battle-hardened Macedonian soldiers, he seemed to be acting more like a god than a simple Macedonian king.

One night in the fall of 328 B.C., during a break in the fighting, Alexander and his officers held a raucous party in Samarkand. After several glasses of wine, Alexander's faithful soldier Cleitus got into a shouting match with his king. Cleitus mocked Alexander for his Persian ways. Alexander was no god, he insisted. He would have died long ago on the battlefield at Granicus if Cleitus himself—a mere mortal—had not saved him. Alexander, Cleitus said, owed his glory to his

ALEXANDER MURDERS CLEITUS, a loyal soldier who had saved his life at the Battle of Granicus. The Lord of Asia seemed to be losing his sanity—and the trust of his Macedonian troops.

men. And yet he made them compete with Persians for an audience with their king.

Blind with anger, Alexander grabbed at a sword, but a bodyguard snatched it away. Friends tried to hustle Cleitus out of the room, but the soldier slipped free. Alexander grabbed a spear and before anyone could stop him, ran it through Cleitus's chest.

As the man who once saved his life lay dying on the floor, Alexander was seized with guilt. He pulled the spear from Cleitus's body and tried to stab himself. Guards stopped him and wrestled him back to his tent. After a day of mourning, Alexander allowed his philosophers to convince him that he should not feel guilty. As "master of the world," they argued, everything he did was just.

Alexander, it seems, was all too willing to believe his philosophers.

In 327 B.C., the Macedonians cornered the last of the rebels in a mountain fortress known as the Rock of Chorienes. When the rebel leader surrendered,

Alexander ascended the rock in triumph. He brought with him a young woman named Roxane, the daughter of a Sogdian nobleman who had recently surrendered to the Macedonians. There, at the summit of the conquered rock, Alexander married his Sogdian bride.

Alexander's men were already disheartened by the killings of Parmenion, Philotas, and Cleitus. Now some of them began to grumble about the marriage. How could their king marry a "barbarian"? She wasn't even a princess!

Alexander brushed aside their criticism. He seemed determined to impose a new vision on his empire. During his march through Asia, he had always respected local customs and religious practices. Now, in order to knit his far-flung empire together, he wanted its diverse cultures and peoples to mingle and combine.

He ordered his men to follow the Persian practice of kneeling at the king's feet. Hephaestion managed to convince many of the Macedonian nobles to follow the order. But the philosopher Callisthenes refused. As the king's official historian, it had been Callisthenes's job to celebrate Alexander's accomplishments. Now he could no longer support his king.

Alexander's revenge came swiftly. He accused Callisthenes of plotting to kill him. He even implied that Aristotle, the historian's uncle, had been in on the conspiracy. Callisthenes died in prison before Alexander could send him back to Greece for trial.

The Lord of Asia had begun to find enemies everywhere, real and imagined. He stayed up long into the night, drinking wine with friends. Often, he lashed out in drunken anger at the slightest insult and then sunk into depression for days on end.

"Stillness and silence born of fear held fast all who were in his presence," wrote the ancient Greek historian Ephippus. "For he was intolerable, and murderous, reputed in fact to be melancholy mad."

# CHAPTER 16

# Toward the Endless Ocean

Alexander pushes into India,
searching for THE EDGE
OF THE WORLD.

FROM SOGDIA, ALEXANDER LOOKED EAST into the unknown. Greek historians had written about the kingdoms of India, but their tales were based on rumors. Greek gods had supposedly traveled in India, but Alexander knew no mortals who had been there. It was said to be a land of cannibals and burrowing ants that dug golden sand from the desert. According to Aristotle, India was the easternmost land in the world. Beyond it lay the Endless Ocean at the edge of the earth. Alexander was determined to press on until his empire reached its shores.

From the mountains of central Asia, Alexander led his men through winding passes down into the humid warmth of India. He made alliances with local leaders who were willing to join him. Those who resisted were quickly overrun.

The Macedonian army crossed the great Indus River and arrived at the waters of the Jhelum River in May 326 B.C. The sight on the far bank must have given even the most rugged soldier pause. The Indian king Porus had positioned thousands of soldiers on the bank. In their midst stood 200 elephants, armored for battle and trumpeting into the sky.

Alexander surveyed the situation. He didn't dare cross the river and attack the Indians directly—he knew that the elephants would panic his horses. Instead, he faked a series of attacks to distract Porus. Then,

THE MACEDONIAN CAVALRY battles a squadron of
Indian war elephants at the Jhelum River. During the battle,
the elephants panicked, killing many Indian soldiers.

when night fell, Alexander led a large force upriver to find another place to cross. Just before dawn, he loaded his men onto boats, rafts, and straw-filled tents, and started across the river.

Porus was slow to respond, and by the time he moved his force upriver, Alexander was fully prepared. He forced the Indian cavalry against the line of elephants. Then his foot soldiers advanced into the chaos with battle axes. They swarmed the elephants, hacking at the legs of the massive beasts. The elephants panicked and trampled the Indian soldiers behind them as they fled.

The battle raged for eight hours, leaving thousands dead in the mud. As his army evaporated around him, King Porus stood on his elephant and flung spears until he slid off, weak from loss of blood.

Alexander was so impressed with his rival's courage that he invited the Indian king into an alliance. When Porus recovered from his wounds, Alexander said, he could not only keep his kingdom but add to it the lands that they would conquer together.

Porus instructed his people to welcome Alexander and his army, and the Macedonians spent two months along the Jhelum River. But despite the hospitality of the Indians, Alexander's men were miserable. The relentless rains of the monsoon season beat down on them. Clothing grew moldy and armor rusted. The soldiers had to sleep in hammocks to escape the mud. Deadly snakes lurked on the ground below. Tropical diseases began to take their toll.

At the height of summer, Alexander mobilized his troops again and set off to the east. For the first time since leaving Macedonia, he traveled without Bucephalus. His beloved horse had died, sending Alexander into mourning for days. But he was as determined as ever to reach the shores of the Endless Ocean.

His men, however, had finally had enough. For eight years they had followed Alexander without a hint of mutiny. But on the west bank of the Beas River, 150 miles east of the Jhelum, a veteran officer named

Coenus gathered his nerve. He stood up to confront his king.

The officers and their men had all accomplished amazing feats together, Coenus said. But their luck could run out at any moment. "Every man . . . longs to see his parents again . . . or his wife, or his children," Coenus declared. "All are yearning for the familiar earth of home."

The tired officers broke into applause.

Alexander retreated to his tent for three days, hoping his men would reconsider. When no one gave in, he called for his fortune-tellers and asked whether it was wise to cross the Beas River and march eastward. They gave him the answer he needed to save face.

Alexander sent for his officers and announced that the signs were unfavorable. He had decided to withdraw.

"One can imagine the shouts of joy," Arrian writes.

After eight years of constant warfare, Alexander's men were going home.

# CHAPTER 17

# Death March

## Heading homeward, the king MAKES A DANGEROUS CHOICE.

ALEXANDER RETURNED TO THE JHELUM River, where he had left a corps of engineers hard at work building ships out of native cedar and fir. In November 326 B.C., he and his army set out down the river in 2,000 boats, including a fleet of galleys each powered by 30 oars.

The weary Macedonians headed south toward the Arabian Sea, where they would turn west and return to Babylon. A month into the journey, they met fierce resistance from a tribe known as the Mallians.

Alexander chased them into the great fortress of Multan. There, as Coenus had warned, his luck almost ran out.

At the dawn of a winter morning, Alexander tried to rally his troops to storm the fortress. Tired and disgruntled, the soldiers made no progress, forcing Alexander to lead the charge himself. He grabbed a siege ladder and climbed the wall, followed by three of his men. Just as they reached the top, the ladder broke, leaving them isolated on the fortress wall.

Alexander and his three comrades leaped into the fort and were immediately swarmed by the Mallians. The Macedonians fought the attackers off until an arrow found its way through Alexander's armor and into his chest. As the king fell, one of his men took the shield of Achilles from his hand and protected him for as long as he could.

Finally, the Macedonians battered their way through the fortress gates. They found their king nearly dead from a punctured lung. In a bloody rage, Alexander's men massacred everyone in the fort.

After being carried back to camp, Alexander somehow fought back from the edge of death. He led his men south to the Arabian Sea, and then west overland toward the heart of Persia. By October 325 B.C., they stood at the edge of a murderous wasteland—the blistering, empty Gedrosian Desert.

Alexander then made a decision so reckless that it seemed he was trying to punish his men for their mutiny on the Beas River. The Lord of Asia took his army straight into the desolate dunes. Following the infantry and cavalry came all those who traveled with the army—engineers, scholars, doctors, and others.

Some 50,000 people started across a 600-mile desert that offered almost no water or food. When the survivors emerged, 500 miles east of Persepolis, as many as 10,000 of their companions had died.

Alexander was among those who made it. But his luck was about to run out, once and for all.

# CHAPTER 18

# Final Battles

## The short and astonishing career of a world conqueror COMES TO AN END.

IN FEBRUARY 324 B.C., ALEXANDER LED what remained of his army through Persepolis and into Susa. His empire now stretched 4,000 miles, from Greece in the west to India in the east.

But the news from his far-flung lands was not good. Nearly half of the satrapies in the empire were close to outright rebellion. Alexander acted quickly and ruthlessly. He summoned 13 of his 20 satraps. Six of them were executed, and two more were replaced.

ALEXANDER AT THE FEAST for his wedding to
Stateira, a daughter of the late Darius III. Alexander had also
ordered 90 of his Macedonian officers to take Persian brides.

Alexander was still determined to knit together
the diverse peoples of his empire. He ordered at least
90 of his Macedonian officers to marry Persian women.
Alexander himself married one of Darius's daughters,
Stateira. He joined his wife's sister with Hephaestion.
The weddings took place in a single Persian-style
ceremony before 9,000 spectators.

Alexander also replaced battle-hardened Macedonian
soldiers with 30,000 young Persian recruits. Despite

the fact that his soldiers had asked to go home, they were "nearly mad with rage and jealousy," according to Plutarch.

With his army refreshed, Alexander began making new war plans. The restless warrior set his sights on the rich kingdom of Arabia to the south and even on Europe, where he envisioned marching as far west as Britain.

Before mobilizing once again, Alexander escaped the summer heat by moving his court to the mountain city of Ecbatana. He distracted himself with athletic games and performances by a traveling troupe of actors from Greece.

Amid the revelry, Hephaestion became gravely ill. A doctor told him to rest, but Alexander's lifelong companion continued to drink. In a few days, he was dead.

Alexander, who had witnessed the death of thousands on the battlefield, "went out of his mind with grief," Plutarch says. The king ordered the doctor crucified. He cut off his own hair in mourning and lay

ALEXANDER WAS DEVASTATED by the death of his friend
Hephaestion. The king had Babylon's protective walls demolished
and used the bricks to build a vast funeral pyre.

on Hephaestion's body, weeping, for 24 hours. When
he returned to Babylon, he built a magnificent 200-foot
funeral pyre and had it set ablaze.

With the loss of Hephaestion, Alexander seemed
to lose confidence in the gods. According to Plutarch,
he "grew downhearted" and "suspicious of his friends."

Near the end of May, Alexander presided over a
series of banquets with his officers, drinking heavily

MACEDONIANS WEEP as Alexander rests on his deathbed. The king had named no successor, and civil wars would soon split his empire into pieces.

for several nights in a row. Then he came down with a terrible fever. Ravaged by countless wounds from a lifetime of war, his body failed quickly. On June 9, several of his Companions spent the night in the temple of Bel, praying to a foreign god to spare their king's life.

The next day, Alexander the Great, ruler of Greece and Lord of Asia, died. He was four months short of his thirty-third birthday.

## *Wicked?*

More than 2,300 years after his violent and dramatic life, Alexander the Great lives on as a character in the world's imagination. Famous generals, from Julius Caesar to Napoleon, have studied and idolized his military conquests. Stories about him appear in the literature of nearly 80 countries. In hundreds of folktales, he is a king, a devil, a hero, a destroyer. In real life, he was all of these things.

Alexander's biggest accomplishment was to open the world to a great mingling of cultures. He founded new centers of trade where people from Europe, the Middle East, Persia, India, and eventually China, came together to exchange goods and ideas. Greek settlers fanned out across Asia, bringing their language and customs with them. They inspired Greek-style theaters and libraries with Greek texts as far east as present-day Afghanistan. Gigantic Greek altars rose on the shores

ALEXANDER THE GREAT CONQUERED lands from
Greece to Egypt to India. He never lost a battle and fought on
the front lines alongside his men. But 12 years of constant warfare
ruined his body and his mind and wiped out nearly an entire
generation of Macedonian warriors.

of the Beas River in India. Athletes and actors traveled to Greek-style competitions all across Asia. Buddhist monks from India even brought their faith all the way to Syria.

Alexander envisioned an interconnected world, and he used his power to realize his dream. He minted coins to create a standard currency so merchants from all over the world could trade with each other. He respected local beliefs and religious rituals wherever he went. He welcomed foreigners into his government and his family, hoping to produce a racially diverse elite that would govern a united Asia for generations after his death.

There is no question that Alexander was ahead of his time in his cultural vision. But he was as merciless as anyone when it came to extending and protecting his power—and infinitely more effective. During his decade-long rampage through Asia, Alexander founded some 70 cities, but destroyed dozens as well. His army may have killed between 500,000 and 750,000 people.

He probably sold another half million into slavery. At least half of those enslaved were women and children.

Alexander's path of destruction extended 11,250 miles through the Middle East, modern-day Iraq, Iran, Afghanistan, Pakistan, and India. Along the way, he grew convinced that he was the son of a god, destined to gain limitless power on earth. When he began to act like a divine emperor, he alienated many of his Macedonian comrades. When his critics dared to defy him, he lashed out ruthlessly, executing many of his closest allies.

Alexander's rages led ancient historians to wonder whether he had descended into madness. In modern terms, he was probably an alcoholic. He may also have had bipolar disorder, doomed to swing between dazzling displays of energy and deep plunges into depression.

In the end, there is no arguing that Alexander accomplished more in 33 years than anyone would think possible. For that, he is remembered, 23 centuries after his death, as the greatest warrior who ever lived, Alexander the Great.

# Timeline of Terror

**356**

**356:** Alexander is born in Macedonia.

**343:** The philosopher Aristotle begins tutoring Alexander.

**338:** Alexander leads a crucial charge as his father, King Philip II, defeats Greek city-states at the Battle of Chaeronea.

**336:** King Philip is assassinated. At 20, Alexander becomes ruler of Macedonia.

**335:** Alexander subdues tribal powers to the north and then destroys the rebellious Greek city-state of Thebes.

**334:** Alexander leads his army into Asia. At the Battle of Granicus, he defeats a Persian army.

**332:** Alexander crushes Tyre and Gaza; he then marches into Egypt and is named the new pharaoh.

**331:** At the Battle of Gaugamela, Alexander's forces destroy the last Persian army. Alexander takes possession of Babylon, the Persian capital.

**330:** Alexander sacks Persepolis. Darius is killed by one of his own satraps.

**328:** Alexander murders Cleitus, one of his longest-serving officers.

**327:** Alexander marries Roxane, the daughter of a nobleman in the Persian Empire.

**326:** In India, Alexander defeats King Porus and his war elephants. Alexander's troops then refuse to go farther east.

**325:** Alexander orders his army to march through the Gedrosian Desert.

**323:** Not quite 33 years old, Alexander dies.

**323**

# GLOSSARY

assassinate (uh-SASS-uh-nate) *verb* to murder someone who is well-known or important

barbarian (bar-BAIR-ee-uhn) *noun* someone who is considered uncultured or brutish

battalion (buh-TAL-yun) *noun* a large unit of soldiers

battering ram (BAT-ur-ing RAM) *noun* a wooden weapon on wheels used to break down city walls in ancient times

bipolar disorder (bye-POH-lur dis-OR-dur) *noun* a psychological disorder marked by alternating moods of depression and elation

breakout (BRAYK-out) *noun* a military charge to break free from a surrounding army

catapult (CAT-uh-puhlt) *noun* a huge weapon, similar to a large slingshot, used for firing rocks or metal arrows over fortress walls

cavalry (KAV-uhl-ree) *noun* soldiers who ride on horseback

chariot (CHA-ree-uht) *noun* a small vehicle pulled by a horse, used in ancient times in battles or for racing

city-state (SIT-ee STATE) *noun* a city that with its surrounding territory forms an independent state

Companion Cavalry (kuhm-PAN-yuhn KAV-uhl-ree) *noun* the elite cavalry of the Macedonian army during the time of Alexander the Great

democracy (di-MOK-ruh-see) *noun* a system of government in which the decisions are made by the people

empire (EM-pire) *noun* a group of regions that have the same ruler

feud (FYOOD) *verb* to quarrel bitterly

illiterate (i-LIT-ur-it) *adjective* not able to read

infantry (IN-fuhn-tree) *noun* the part of an army that fights on foot invincible (in-VIN-suh-buhl) *adjective* not able to be beaten or defeated

javelin (JAV-uh-luhn) *noun* a light throwing spear

liberator (LIB-uhr-ay-tuhr) *noun* someone who sets someone else free

melancholy (MEL-uhn-kol-ee) *adjective* extremely depressed

mercenary (MUR-suh-ner-ee) *noun* a soldier who is paid to fight for a foreign army

oasis (oh-AY-siss) *noun* a place in the desert where there is water and plants grow

oracle (OR-uh-kuhl) *noun* in ancient times, a priest who was a mouthpiece for a god

peninsula (puh-NIN-suh-luh) *noun* a piece of land that sticks out from a larger land mass and is almost completely surrounded by water

phalanx (FAL-anks) *noun* in ancient Greece and Macedonia, a body of infantry with long spears, moving in close formation

pike (PIKE) *noun* a very long stabbing spear that is held with both hands

province (PROV-uhnss) *noun* a district or region of some countries

relentless (ri-LENT-liss) *adjective* endlessly determined

satrap (SA-trap) *noun* a governor of a province in ancient Persia

satrapy (SA-truh-pee) *noun* the territory governed by a satrap

siege engine (SEEJ EN-jin) *noun* a device, such as a battering ram or siege tower, used to destroy or surmount fortress walls

strategist (STRAT-uh-jist) *noun* a person who develops a plan for winning a military battle or achieving a goal

winch (WINCH) *noun* a machine that lifts or pulls heavy objects

# FIND OUT MORE

*Here are some books and websites with more information about Alexander the Great and his times.*

## BOOKS

Crompton, Samuel Willard. **Alexander the Great (Ancient World Leaders)**. Philadelphia: Chelsea House, 2003. (110 pages) *Describes the life and accomplishments of Alexander the Great.*

Gunther, John. **Alexander the Great**. New York: Sterling, 2007. (159 pages) *A well-written biography of Alexander the Great by famed historian John Gunther.*

Morley, Jacqueline. **You Wouldn't Want to Be in Alexander the Great's Army! Miles You'd Rather Not March**. New York: Franklin Watts, 2005. (32 pages) *This book humorously explores the unpleasant details of being a soldier in Alexander the Great's army.*

Pearson, Anne. **Ancient Greece (DK Eyewitness Books)**. New York: DK Publishing, 2007. (72 pages) *A colorful and informative look at the history, people, and customs of Ancient Greece.*

## WEBSITES

http://encarta.msn.com/encyclopedia_761564408/Alexander_the_Great.html
*MSN Encarta's online encyclopedia article about Alexander the Great.*

http://www.ac.wwu.edu/~stephan/Animation/alexander.html
*On this site, you can trace Alexander's conquests on two maps, one of them animated.*

http://www.hermitagemuseum.org/html_En/04/2007/hm4_1_154.html
*Learn about fascinating ancient artifacts from* Alexander the Great, The Road to the East, *a 2007 exhibition at the Hermitage Museum in St. Petersburg.*

http://www.historyforkids.org/learn/greeks/history/alexander.htm
*This interesting article on Alexander the Great is from* Kidipede, *a fun online history resource sponsored by Portland State University.*

http://www.pbs.org/howartmadetheworld/episodes/persuasion/alexander
*The online companion to the PBS series* How Art Made the World *includes this page on Alexander the Great's use of portraiture to create a political image for himself*

**For Grolier subscribers:**
http://go.grolier.com/ **searches:** Alexander the Great; Greece, Ancient; Aristotle; Persia, Ancient; Darius; Egypt, Ancient; Ancient Civilizations

# INDEX

# Author's Note and Bibliography

For me, the fun of working on Alexander's incredible story really got going when I dug into the ancient chronicles of his life and campaigns. Each chronicler has his or her own viewpoint. I often had to sift through them, separating what might be myth or legend from what seemed true. The details in these accounts helped me to bring Alexander to life.

There is no other story quite like Alexander's. I hope you've enjoyed reading it as much as I did writing it.

The following sources have been the most useful in writing this book.

Ancient historians:

Arrian, a Greek who lived in the second century A.D. **The Campaigns of Alexander.** London: Penguin Books, 1971.

Curtius, a Roman of the first century A.D. **The History of Alexander.** London: Penguin Books, 1984.

Plutarch, a Greek historian of the first century A.D. **Selected Lives and Essays.** New York: Walter J. Black, 1951.


Modern historians:

Cartledge, Paul. **Alexander the Great.** New York: The Overlook Press, 2004.

Fildes, Alan and Joann Fletcher. **Alexander the Great: Son of the Gods.** Los Angeles: Getty Publications, 2002.

Stoneman, Richard. **Alexander the Great: A Life in Legend.** New Haven, Conn.: Yale University Press, 2008.

Wood, Michael. **In the Footsteps of Alexander the Great.** Berkeley: University of California Press, 2001.

—Doug Wilhelm